You're Finally Over 30 When . . .

* You use a walkman because it's the only way you can understand the words

* You think being good in bed refers to overcoming your insomnia

* You don't throw away your fat clothes because you've accepted that life is cyclical

* You can't party for 24 hours and live to tell about it

* You realize that 40 isn't all that old

"Moisturizer Is My Religion"

or You're Finally Over 30 When...

by Victoria Black

BALLANTINE BOOKS • NEW YORK

Library of Congress Catalog Card Number: 83-91219

ISBN 0-345-31387-9

Manufactured in the United States of America

First Edition: March 1984

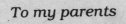

To my parents

TABLE OF
CONTENTS

DATING
&
RELATIONSHIPS

You're Finally Over 30 When . . .

You realize that if you date a 42-year-old man, he's no longer robbing the cradle.

●

You don't solicit three opinions before you break up with him.

1

You don't use the "my aunt gave me her two tickets" gambit if you want to ask a guy out.

•

You don't hate his ex-girlfriends until you meet them.

•

You have the willpower to decline that first date with the gorgeous SOB.

•

You realize that you really are better off without him.

•

You don't double date.

•

That romantic weekend with your new flame means a Little League game and a wienie roast with his kids.

•

The only single bars you like are Hershey's.

You don't pretend to like his friends.

●

You find a man's robe in your closet and can't remember to whom it belonged.

●

You don't get up with him just to make breakfast.

●

You'd rather have him successful than handsome.

●

You don't want to meet his relatives.

●

You realize that newly divorced men are not capable of rational thought.

●

Someone *else* is the other woman.

●

Men who are not gay, not married and not neurotic are not around.

3

You distrust men who espouse feminism but don't know how to make coffee.

●

Serial monogamy seems a lot more promising than marriage.

●

You don't buy new negligees at the start of an affair.

●

You don't buy old clichés at the end of an affair.

●

You discover that ex-wives have their reasons.

●

You realize that a shared passion for The Who does not provide a sound basis for moving in together.

●

Old flames provide no heat but plenty of illumination.

You prefer to be the one who wears earrings.

●

You adore him.

●

You detest him.

●

You accept your contradictory nature.

●

You listen when friends who have been involved with married men tell you not to.

●

You make *him* give up *his* apartment when you decide to live together.

●

You realize that bisexuals aren't worth it—his old girlfriends are bad enough.

●

You expect fidelity only from your stereo.

You realize that the landing's a lot harder when you've been swept off your feet.

●

Your friends don't get married in the park anymore.

●

You've learned that breaking up is hard to do, but dividing the record collection is impossible.

FOOD

You're Finally Over 30 When . . .

You don't approach a Sara Lee cheese-cake as if it were Mt. Everest—you don't eat it all just because it's there.

●

You accept that MacDonald's provides an occasional meal and not a way of life.

You eat sushi without thinking of Flipper.

●

You no longer consider salad a finger food.

●

You discover that the chocolate chip cookie is not a basic food group.

●

All the vegetables you would never eat cooked you now eat raw.

●

You don't buy Crackerjacks for the prize.

●

You use your fondue pot as a planter.

●

You eat cereals high in bran content instead of Sugar-Frosted Crispios.

●

You realize that brunch is not an internationally recognized meal.

You admit that yogurt is no substitute for sour cream.

●

You discover that 5¢ candy bars now cost 30¢, have half the weight, and add twice the girth.

●

You've eaten enough quiche and brie to sink the Normandy.

●

You don't eat pizza at midnight because you know you'll pay for it at three.

●

You can deftly pretend that you're serving nouvelle cuisine when, in truth, you just don't have enough to go around.

●

You know that home-cooked meals taste best cooked in other people's homes.

●

You're familiar with more in the pasta family than spaghetti.

Your supermarket cart contains at least 12% protein.

●

You've memorized the phone numbers of all restaurants with 24-hour delivery.

●

You drink decaffeinated coffee after dinner.

●

You stop opening stubborn pistachios with your teeth, because it might break your crown.

●

You have considered turning the kitchen into a den. *or* You have considered expanding your kitchen into your bedroom.

●

You discover that your Cuisinart is good for more than superior frozen margaritas.

●

You have, and use, a wine rack . . . and none of the wines have screw caps.

MUSIC

You're Finally Over 30 When . . .

You think that new wave is something a Tony twin might have.

•

You use a Sony Walkman because that's the only way you can understand the words.

You don't buy albums for their posters.

●

No one has to ask you to turn down your stereo.

●

You've caught yourself, at least once, thinking that the lyrics to love songs are profound.

●

You have serious doubts about the pleasures of slam dancing.

●

You no longer call the radio request line.

●

You wait for the greatest hits album before you buy.

●

You wish you had stuck with the piano.

●

You discover that Cole Porter and George

Gershwin have a lot more staying power than the Strawberry Alarm Clock.

●

You can't name the Top 10.

●

You can't name the Top 5.

●

You remember when Dick Clark was younger than you are now.

●

The only hard rock you like is four carats.

●

You find that most of your record collection falls into the "oldies but goodies" category.

●

You can't remember the names of all the Beatles' old girlfriends and wives.

●

You'd rather attend a storewide sale than a Stones concert.

SHELTER

You're finally Over 30 When . . .

You clean your apartment because you like it that way and not because Queen Elizabeth is coming for brunch.

●

You organize things so you can "save steps."

You own your own vacuum cleaner.

●

You only serve white wine because red stains.

●

You own more than two matching dinner plates.

●

You change your linens every week even when you're the only one who sees them.

●

You have to choose between a dishwasher and a fireplace and have a hard time deciding.

●

You buy toilet paper before it runs out so that you don't have to steal a roll from the office john.

●

You polish your silver even before it turns black.

You keep extra lightbulbs and batteries.

●

You don't name your plants.

●

You always refill the ice cube tray and can open it by yourself.

●

You don't volunteer your home for meetings.

●

You enjoy browsing in hardware stores more than in head shops.

●

You don't give out your housekey without fingerprints, blood test, and proof of citizenship.

●

You've purchased more furnishings than you've been given.

●

You've cleaned your oven at least once.

You've stopped waiting for someone to come over who will offer to take out the garbage.

●

You realize that your next move will require professional movers.

●

You never forget to lock the front door— you only think you forgot.

●

Your freezer doesn't look like the coming ice age has arrived.

●

You don't look in the closet for burglars (unless it's thundering and very late).

●

You no longer feel guilty about hiring a "cleaning person."

SPORTS

You're Finally Over 30 When . . .

You realize that at some point you're going to have to learn what a "down" is—aside from a drug.

●

You realize that Chris Evert is younger than you.

You think of a lap as something to sit on, not swim.

●

You've given up downhill for cross-country skiing.

●

You accept that the only way you'll make it to the Olympics is with a ticket.

●

You donate your skateboard to Goodwill.

●

You won't go camping without an air mattress, full mosquito netting, and a bottle of good brandy.

●

You hate overtime.

●

Golf no longer seems silly.

●

You prefer Connors to McEnroe.

You know never to play mixed doubles with the man you love.

●

Wearing running clothes is more a matter of comfort than chic.

●

You have no qualms about beating him in straight sets, but you can also pretend to lose graciously.

●

You accept that there is no such thing as a softball game played "just for fun."

●

You realize that if you slide into third, you'll limp home.

●

Your stockings run faster than you do.

CLOTHING

You're Finally Over 30 When . . .

You admit that you're more comfortable in your flannel nightgown.

●

You don't lie to yourself that one piece suits are sexier than bikinis.

You concede that your white pants didn't shrink from sitting in the closet all winter.

●

You don't throw away your fat clothes— you have accepted that life is cyclical.

●

You always buy more than one pair of stockings at a time.

●

You wear neither t-shirts nor underwear which proclaim your philosophical beliefs.

●

You've also traded in the ones with days of the week for something sheer and black.

●

You buy bathing suits meant for swimming.

●

You know that the saleswoman says "It looks marvelous on you" to everyone.

You don't wear your suede shoes if it looks like rain.

•

You don't buy clothes with the intention of returning them.

•

You refuse to wear his 'n her anything.

•

You can remember when someone you knew wore harlequin glasses.

•

Your bedroom slippers don't look like bunnies.

•

You own one hundred fifty pairs of earrings and three backs.

•

The ratio between your costume jewelry and the real stuff is narrowing.

You don't buy a blouse unless it goes with something.

●

Your pocketbook could sustain life for three days.

●

You prefer quality to quantity.

●

You know that just because the invitation says "dress casual," it doesn't necessarily mean jeans.

●

You realize that there's a lot to be said for classic-style clothing.

ENTERTAINMENT

You're Finally Over 30 When . . .

You look up answers to crossword puzzles without guilt—if you don't know the African antelope by now, you never will.

●

You go to the movies alone on a Saturday night without sunglasses and a hat.

You freely admit that you watch more on TV than "M*A*S*H" reruns and PBS.

●

You read the editorial page.

●

You know the only purpose of self-improvement books is holding down curled carpet edges.

●

You stop filling out the self-analysis quizzes in magazines because you already know your personality/body type.

●

You shelve *Remembrance of Things Past* after being on page 27 for five years.

●

You've fulfilled your Book-of-the-Month Club commitment.

●

You spend more quarters at the laundromat than the video arcade.

26

You pretend that you don't read *Cosmo*.

●

You read all the books you buy.

●

You pretend that you don't like ethnic jokes.

●

You prefer a quiet dinner party for ten to a pretzel and beer bash for fifty.

●

You go to more dinner parties than pot parties.

●

Sometimes you buy hardcovers.

●

You only listen to FM radio.

●

You've walked out at intermission at least once.

You read the reviews before you go to the movie.

●

You see the inherent danger of roller coasters.

●

(A) Scott Fitzgerald, (B) Sylvia Plath, or (C) Virginia Woolf is not your favorite author.

●

You watch the State of the Union speech instead of the old movie on channel 5.

●

You own a medical reference book.

●

You use it with increasing frequency.

●

You've attended a surprise party where someone was actually surprised.

28

You record the "Late Late Show" instead of staying up all night.

●

You always bring a gift for the hostess.

●

You don't mind going to the party without a date.

●

You don't mind leaving the party without a date.

●

You sometimes long for movies that end happily ever after.

●

You can't party for 24 hours straight and live to talk about it.

●

You'd rather stay home on New Year's Eve than go out on a blind date.

WORK

You're Finally Over 30 When . . .

You don't call in sick just because it's a perfect beach day.

●

You don't give your secretary a play-by-play of your current relationship.

Your professional association calls you a "member of long standing."

●

You don't throw out the company pamphlet on the pension plan.

●

Your bulletin board has more memos than memorabilia.

●

You've used your medical plan at least once.

●

You don't get drunk with people from the office.

●

You learn that no response is necessary to 95% of all interoffice memos.

●

You worry when projects go too smoothly.

You don't throw up before giving major presentations.

●

You're a "contact."

●

You only cry in the ladies' room.

●

You're nice to everybody because you know "you never know."

●

The money is more important than the title.

●

People ask to use you for a reference.

●

You can stop faking your resume.

●

You don't take your briefcase home when you don't have any work.

You don't wear a string bikini at the national sales meeting.

●

You know there is no such thing as a secret office affair.

●

You're someone's mentor.

●

In the office at midnight you start thinking about the quality of life.

●

Your office attire brings to mind neither the Pointer sisters nor the Brooks brothers.

●

In case of fire, the first thing you grab is your Rolodex.

●

You think about starting your own business.

You have enough clothes for several rounds of job interviews.

●

You're not afraid to use your expense account.

●

You only like snowstorms that are bad enough to close down the office.

●

You avoid office party planning meetings.

●

You're not impressed by workaholics.

●

You realize that you're not indispensible.

●

You see the names of people you know in trade publications.

●

You've eliminated astronaut and cowgirl from your list of career goals.

COMMUNICATION

You're Finally Over 30 When . . .

Your mother calls and you're not disappointed.

●

You remember to write thank-you notes.

Your signature contains no happy faces.

•

You let him answer your phone.

•

You break chain letters without worrying about it.

•

You don't call him and hang up to see if he really is working late.

•

You always understand the dirty joke.

•

You can lie gracefully.

•

You consider getting "call waiting" and "call forwarding." ·

•

You discover that perception is more important than reality.

36

You occasionally use the word "gay" to mean festive.

●

The phone company never disconnects you for lack of payment.

●

You don't write fan letters.

●

You can refrain from always answering the phone at home.

●

You've learned through bitter experience that 99.4% of the world population cannot keep a secret.

●

You've spelled your first name the same way for at least seven years.

●

You buy an answering machine instead of waiting by the phone.

You've stopped using the cute opening line on the tape.

●

You phone instead of write.

●

You talk about your "space" you're referring to the parking lot.

●

You never expect good news in the mail.

●

You can swear like a pro. But you've got enough restraint to do it only in appropriate situations.

●

You don't use euphemisms for parts of the body.

●

You don't think talking to yourself is weird.

●

You frequently listen to reason.

38

You can make restaurant reservations without stammering.

●

You discover that every cliché has an opposite cliché.

●

You discover that all clichés are true.

●

Your stationery doesn't have pastel animals on it.

●

You don't even open the mail addressed to occupant.

●

You don't like receiving telegrams.

●

You sigh involuntarily.

DRUGS
&
ALCOHOL

You're Finally Over 30 When . . .

Your dealer wears a three-piece suit.

●

You know that discretion is the better part of Valium.

When someone says pot your first thought is of something to cook in.

●

You don't order drinks that contain more than two liquids.

●

You don't drink anything that's rainbow colored.

●

You've learned that there is no remedy for hangovers save death.

●

You don't care if you're the only one who orders a soft drink.

●

You *do* coke instead of drink it.

●

You only do drugs on weekends.

●

You can afford a full ounce.

You're afraid marijuana may not be commercially available in your lifetime.

●

You don't try to grow dope in the kitchen window.

●

When you take a trip a suitcase is involved.

●

Your "personal papers" do not refer to E–Z Widers.

●

You know your limit.

●

You've exceeded it many times.

●

Teatime means Earl Grey.

●

You don't waste good grass in brownies.

You discover that tea and sympathy aren't as soothing as scotch and sympathy.

●

You drink brandy instead of cocoa when you can't sleep.

●

You don't think a 99¢ bottle of wine is a good buy.

●

You don't buy from anyone you don't know.

●

Pot luck refers to food.

●

You believe that drinks topped by little umbrellas should only be served to small, wet people.

HEALTH

You're Finally Over 30 When . . .

You still bask in the sun all summer, but you have begun to worry about it.

●

Your thighs have a life of their own.

You stay in bed when you're sick.

●

Your doctor bills are larger than your phone bills.

●

You go to the gynecologist for a check-up even if you don't need birth control.

●

You realize that having only diet soda, mustard, and taco sauce in the fridge is not the path to better nutrition.

●

You know your blood pressure.

●

You make dentist appointments.

●

You keep dentist appointments.

●

You skip your warm-up exercises and you pay for it.

You turn down the health club's five-year contract and pay as you go—knowing it will result in a savings of thousands.

●

You don't think plastic surgery is vain.

●

The smoke alarm is the only thing that can get you out of bed before noon on Sunday.

●

You don't fall asleep with your contacts.

●

Pimples cause distress—wrinkles cause despair—liver spots cause disbelief.

●

You don't know anyone who has mono.

●

You use the hot tub for easing sore muscles.

●

You look for signs that your smoker's hack is turning into emphysema.

46

People prefer their casts unsigned.

●

You worry about periodontia instead of orthodontia.

●

You're at peace with your freckles.

●

You have chronic _____ trouble (fill in a body part).

●

You discover that you once babysat for your dermatologist.

GROOMING

You're Finally Over 30 When . . .

You admit that those hairs are gray and not just sun-bleached.

●

Applying moisturizer two times a day is not just a routine but a religion.

Your friends wouldn't recognize you without your makeup.

●

You don't tell your hairdresser everything.

●

You realize that no one else notices the pimple on your forehead.

●

Your hair color remains the same through two major holidays.

●

There's more makeup in the bathroom than food in the kitchen.

●

You'd rather give up your cat than your hair blower.

●

You don't spend $85.00 with the makeup demonstrator because you know you'll wind up using only the lipstick.

You don't shut yourself in for a week after a bad haircut.

●

You will not dye your hair green under any circumstances.

●

You have your shoes repaired before the heels reach a 45 degree angle.

●

You almost always remove your makeup before you go to bed.

●

Your perfume isn't sold by the quart.

●

You don't wear nail polish in any shade approaching green, black, or blue.

●

Your leg hair never reaches braiding length.

You sew your fallen hems instead of taping them.

•

You do your laundry before you completely run out of underwear.

•

You firmly believe that all ironing is best left to professionals.

MONEY

You're Finally Over 30 When . . .

Your assets include more than thick eye-lashes and straight teeth.

●

You have a good idea of how much is in your checking account.

You don't think credit cards are better than cash.

●

You usually have more than $5.00 left by the next payday.

●

You keep your canceled checks.

●

You know more about real estate than the rent on Marvin Gardens.

●

You have your own accountant.

●

You comparison-shop for major purchases.

●

You make major purchases.

●

You know that balloon payments aren't for party supplies.

53

IRA brings to mind April 15th instead of March 17th.

●

You develop more than a passing interest in tax shelters.

●

You actually maintain the bank's required minimum balance.

●

You leave a poor tip for poor service.

●

Your credit card applications are always approved.

●

They solicit you as a customer.

●

You worry that Social Security funds may run out by the time you're eligible.

●

You accept that purchasing a $100.00

skirt for $60.00 does not give you an extra $40.00 to buy a matching blouse.

●

Over-the-counter does not refer to lunch at the deli.

PARENTS

You're Finally Over 30 When . . .

You find that your conversation is sprinkled with phrases that sound uncannily like your mother.

●

You don't feel the compulsion to tell your mother about your more interesting exploits.

You trust your parents' judgment more than the man in the street's.

●

You don't get upset when you ask your mother for the truth and she tells you.

●

You care what your parents think, but it doesn't change your mind.

●

You freely admit that you like your parents.

●

The only time you sleep in a twin bed is at your parents'.

●

Your parents don't refer to your peers as "your little friends."

●

Your parents don't give allowances—they make them.

The only people you address by their last names are your parents' friends.

●

You understand why your mother can't stand her relatives.

●

Your father doesn't let you beat him at tennis.

●

Your parents ask your advice.

●

You laugh at the same jokes.

●

You don't "break your parents' hearts" on a regular basis.

●

You have figured out that parents only have as much authority as you allow them.

Your parents acknowledge that you have a sex life.

●

You acknowledge that your parents have a sex life.

SCHOOL

You're Finally Over 30 When . . .

You realize that when your baby sister says she's got to get to school it's to pick up her kid.

●

You go to your college reunion not to renew old friendships but to measure everyone on your success scale.

You scan the obit section of the alumni news.

●

Life has confirmed that there really never *was* any reason to learn geometry.

●

You can't find your high school yearbook . . . and you don't care.

●

You hear that your high school football team's star player has just graduated to Methadone.

●

Your college major has no bearing on your life.

●

You once knew how to do long division without a calculator.

●

You've lost your writer's callous.

You have no intention of learning the metric system.

●

You can't remember your SAT scores.

●

You think a heavy course load refers to a big dinner.

●

You've accepted that "Christmas vacation" means two days off.

●

You no longer have nightmares about being late for exams.

●

Someone says "mixers" you think of soda water and gingerale.

●

You've overcome the compulsion to underline your books in yellow.

You can't get a bridge game together at two in the morning.

●

You remember when business majors had to take typing.

●

You forget the difference between "ibid" and "idem."

SEX

You're Finally Over 30 When . . .

You refrain from using massage oil because it stains the sheets.

●

You don't know any virgins personally.

You can say no without making excuses.

●

You can say yes without making excuses.

●

You discover that hand size, thumb size, and nose size are just that.

●

"Kinky" means the lights on and the stereo off.

●

You're not embarrassed to admit that you prefer the bed over the bathtub.

●

You eat garlic even if your date doesn't.

●

You hang up your clothes first.

●

Sometimes you'd rather just sleep.

"Pulling a fast one" is not necessarily funny.

●

You always remember to take care of the birth control.

●

You know more people who use diaphragms than pills.

●

You don't ask him about his sexual history.

●

You lie about your sexual history.

●

You buy Mazola to cook with.

●

Snoring is ample reason to call the whole thing off.

●

You ask him to shave first.

You realize that there's a big difference between men who are communicative and men who are communicable.

●

You think about how many calories you're burning.

●

You wait until the "Saturday Night Live" rerun is over.

●

You've learned that *Great Expectations* can lead to a *Bleak House*.

●

You realize that "I hardly know you" is not an excuse but a reason.

●

You remember when you weren't leery of cold sores.

●

Any man with a vasectomy is at least an 8.

You think the only thing that should be laid on the floor is carpeting.

•

You think that being good in bed refers to overcoming your insomnia.

•

Trying a new position means sleeping on the other side.

•

You think public displays of affection should be restricted to animals and children.

•

You think that four on the floor refers to a gearshift.

VACATIONS

You're Finally Over 30 When . . .

Instead of looking for the action, you look for peace and quiet.

●

You travel with prescription drugs only.

You don't bring back dope from the islands.

●

You do use up your liquor quota.

●

You don't expect to meet the light of your life on the plane.

●

You don't expect the pilot to look like Charlton Heston.

●

You don't care if you get the window seat.

●

You don't throw out the pictures from your trip to Antigua just because they make you look fat.

●

Cross-country car trips have lost their charm.

●

You carry traveler's checks.

Your makeup alone could fill a knapsack.

●

You never travel without birth control.

●

Before you leave, you freely acknowledge that you will not wear 25% of what you've packed.

●

You go to Acapulco not for the gold but the silver.

●

You try not to go on vacation when the colleges are out.

●

You'd rather sit in a cave than go to Ft. Lauderdale in the spring.

●

You own matching luggage.

●

In Rome you do as the tourists do.

You can sleep on the eve of a big trip.

●

The true test of any relationship is sharing a suitcase.

TRANSPORTATION

You're Finally Over 30 When . . .

You don't intentionally try to see how far you can drive on empty.

●

You voluntarily fasten your seat belt and lock the doors.

You don't speed without a pretty good reason.

●

You're at least as concerned with M.P.G. as you are with AM/FM.

●

You take cabs at night instead of just walking fast.

●

You always buy more than a dollar's worth of gas.

●

You are beginning to understand what the mechanic is talking about.

●

You always ask for an estimate.

●

You're not afraid to complain that the job was done wrong.

74

You don't use the back seat as a waste basket.

●

You belong to AAA.

●

You pay your parking tickets.

●

You don't have a college sticker on your car.

●

You don't automatically put the windows down and volume up.

●

You don't press all the elevator buttons.

●

You have a basket on your bicycle.

●

You don't participate in elevator races.

You don't mind asking the driver to slow down.

●

You don't consider hitch-hiking a mode of transportation.

●

You don't want to know the cab driver's philosophy of life.

●

You appreciate the benefits of four-door cars

WOMEN'S LIBERATION

You're Finally Over 30 When . . .

You sympathize with Jean Harris.

●

You're grateful that the superwoman image has been debunked.

You use "network" as a verb.

•

At least one friend who once waxed radical lib now waxes kitchen floors.

•

You've begun to regret the dutch treat concept.

•

If he accepts your money, you don't think he's liberated; you think he's cheap.

•

You still call each other "girls," but resent it when others do.

•

You exchange business cards.

•

Friendships don't break up over men.

•

You can't reconcile your feminism with the desire to have the door held open.

You accept that all your friends don't have to like each other.

●

You don't consider spending an evening with women friends as second best to going on a date.

●

You've attended almost as many marriages as a bridesmaid as Elizabeth Taylor has as a bride.

●

You're turned off by men who think that your ERA button means you're an avid baseball fan.

●

You think that all your friends look younger than their age.

ODDS & ENDS

(you realize that everything

can't be categorized)

You're Finally Over 30 When . . .

You don't care what your doorman thinks about your 5:00 A.M. arrival.

●

You wonder if you'll still be called a "baby boomer" when you're sixty.

You admit that your dog actually does belong to the animal kingdom.

●

You don't wake up at 6:00 A.M. on Christmas morning.

●

You don't ask anyone for autographs.

●

You don't ask other people how old they are.

●

You know someone semifamous.

●

You can't cope without your appointment book.

●

You accept your neuroses.

●

You're almost positive that horoscopes are bunk.

You won't let the maitre d' seat you by the kitchen.

●

You don't smoke cigarettes with designs.

●

You know better than to recommend hair-dressers or doctors.

●

You aren't stunned, but still annoyed, when the cashier calls you ma'am.

●

You hear that two of the kids in your bunk the summer you were a counselor are now lawyers.

●

You finally go to jury duty.

●

You know that the actual event will not be as awful as the anxiety that precedes it.

You feel somewhat patriotic when you hear the "Star Spangled Banner."

●

You tend to learn from experience.

●

Your address book looks like it's been through several wars.

●

You assume the worst but are still disappointed when it happens.

●

There's only one candle on your birthday cake—*if* you get a cake.

●

People ask if you've ever been married.

●

Learning the hard way has lost its glamour.

●

You only vote for candidates in major political parties.

Your rationalizing ability is state of the art.

●

You think that superstitions are silly.

●

You don't walk under ladders if you can help it.

●

You think that a nonconformist is someone who orders Perrier without the lime.

●

You don't need a reason to buy yourself flowers.

●

You don't even bother making New Year's resolutions.

●

You realize that you'll probably never join the Peace Corps.

●

You accept that a large portion of the world population views you as a grown-up.

You realize that staying up as late as you want, eating what and when you want, and reading and watching TV as often as you want is just as much fun as you always thought it might be.

●

You're not intimidated by overbearing sales people.

●

You remember when Halloween treat bags didn't resemble mine fields.

●

You find it reassuring to see police around.

●

Your youth has become camp.

●

You love spontaneity as long as you have a little warning.

●

You realize that 40 isn't really all that old.

ABOUT THE AUTHOR

Victoria Black is a graduate of Skidmore College and Fordham University Graduate School of Business. An ex-New Yorker, she now lives in Washington D.C. She has been 29 for several years.